Phonics Focus: sound of ou

THE SCOUT

BY CHRISTINA EARLEY

ILLUSTRATED BY
BELLA RECH

A Blue Marlin Book

Introduction:

Phonics is the relationship between letters and sounds. It is the foundation for reading words, or decoding. A phonogram is a letter or group of letters that represents a sound. Students who practice phonics and sight words become fluent word readers. Having word fluency allows students to build their comprehension skills and become skilled and confident readers.

Activities:

BEFORE READING

Use your finger to underline the key phonogram in each word in the *Words to Read* list on page 3. Then, read the word. For longer words, look for ways to break the word into smaller parts (double letters, word I know, ending, etc.).

DURING READING

Use sticky notes to annotate for understanding. Write questions, make connections, summarize each page after it is read, or draw an emoji that describes how you felt about different parts.

AFTER READING

Share and discuss your sticky notes with an adult or peer who also read the story.

Key Word/Phonogram: scout

Words to Read:

foul	account	outfield
house	breakout	outfits
loud	counter	outhit
mouse	county	outlet
out	crouching	outline
bound	devours	outpost
couch	discount	pouncing
hound	dugouts	printout
mound	fountain	slouches
pouch	Glouster	standouts
scout	grounders	trousers
shouts	inbound	tryouts
south	lookout	workout
spouse	lousy	announcer
sprout	mountain	
trout	mousy	
about	outdoor	

Mr. South is a scout for the Glouster Mountain Lions. He has mousy brown hair. He wears outfits with loud shirts and blue trousers.

He is always on the lookout for breakout players. He travels with his hound dog named Sprout.

Today, Mr. South is bound for the All-County Tryouts. The event is at Mouse Field.

He picks up a printout from the counter. He finds a seat at the outdoor outpost.

He takes out a pouch of supplies. He plugs his computer into an outlet.

First, all players do a workout by running the outline of the field. Then, catchers begin crouching. Fielders are in the outfield pouncing on grounders.

"All players to the dugouts," shouts the announcer. "It is batting time. Which player will outhit all the others?"

Each pitcher gets to stand on the mound. Mr. South uses his counter to keep track of the hits.

Some players are lousy and hit foul balls. Others are standouts. Mr. South takes account of each one.

After the tryouts, Mr. South takes the inbound train back to his house. He devours a trout dinner with his spouse.

Then, he slouches on the couch to watch a show about how to make a fountain for a discount.

Quiz:

1. True or false? Sprout is a hound dog.
2. True or false? Mr. South likes to eat trout.
3. True or false? The players run the outline of the field after batting.
4. What is one character trait that Mr. South has? How do you know?
5. Do you think Mr. South will make a fountain? Why or why not?

Flip the book around for answers!

Answers:
1. True
2. True
3. False
4. Possible answer: He is organized because he has a pouch with his supplies.
5. Possible answer: Yes, because he watches a show about making something so he must like to make things.

Activities:

1. Write a story about your favorite sport or activity.

2. Write a new story using some or all of the "ou" words from this book.

3. Create a vocabulary word map for a word that was new to you. Write the word in the middle of a paper. Surround it with a definition, illustration, sentence, and other words related to the vocabulary word.

4. Make a song to help others learn the sound of "ou."

5. Create a meme about the "ou" key word "scout."

Written by: Christina Earley
Illustrated by: Bella Rech
Design by: Rhea Magaro-Wallace
Editor: Kim Thompson
Educational Consultant: Marie Lemke, M.Ed.
Series Development: James Earley

Library of Congress PCN Data
The Scout (ou) / Christina Earley
Blue Marlin Readers
ISBN 979-8-8873-5300-5 (hard cover)
ISBN 979-8-8873-5385-2 (paperback)
ISBN 979-8-8873-5470-5 (EPUB)
ISBN 979-8-8873-5555-9 (eBook)
Library of Congress Control Number: 2022951104

Printed in the United States of America.

Seahorse Publishing Company
seahorsepub.com

Copyright © 2024 **SEAHORSE PUBLISHING COMPANY**

All rights reserved. No part of this publication may be reproduced, stored in a retrieval system or be transmitted in any form or by any means, electronic, mechanical, photocopying, recording, or otherwise, without the prior written permission of Seahorse Publishing Company.

Published in the United States
Seahorse Publishing
PO Box 771325
Coral Springs, FL 33077